# Foreword

**Left:** Bird's-eye view of Hull by Frank Pettingell 1880.

**Front Cover:** Colin Screeton from the volunteer maintenance crew aboard the berthed Arctic Corsair.

**Back Cover:** "We Are Hull" projected onto the Maritime Museum as part of the Made In Hull programme in the first week of 2017.

The city of Kingston upon Hull has played a leading part in British commercial and political life for over seven hundred years. Its early history as a royal planned town can still be seen in the streets of the Old Town. Its medieval wealth can be felt in the grandeur of its parish churches. It has proud stories to tell of its role in the Civil War and the Second World War, while its docks mark a succession of international trading, from wool and wine to whaling, timber, coal and fish.

Hull City Council and Historic England have produced this booklet to share the stories of this important European city as a legacy of its role as UK City of Culture 2017. Each of the key phases of its history is explained through surviving buildings and places which bring its past to life. Hull is part of the country's busiest port complex and historically was the arrival-point for over a million transmigrants seeking a better life. Its people have every reason to be proud of their city and visitors have much to see. This publication is a guide for residents and visitors alike to Hull's rich history.

The politician Herbert Morrison, one-time High Steward of the city, wrote 'Hull is part of the county of York, but it seems to be sort of a kingdom of its own, with an identity of its own. It is a remarkable place with an individual character'. Foremost for us is the Old Town - the King's Town - truly a sensational place, nestling between the rivers and the old docks. Its quiet streets, paved with stone setts, lead to great museums, pubs and other places of interest. It is a sad fact that too many travellers pass through the city without visiting. This booklet alongside the designation of Hull as a Heritage Action Zone will support us as we build on the successes of City of Culture to ensure that the Old Town becomes once more the busy heart of the city. Its history is the story of all of Hull's citizens, past and present, and should be a shared source of pride and delight.

**Councillor Stephen Brady**
Leader of Hull City Council

**Sir Laurie Magnus**
Chair of Historic England

# Introduction

The city of Hull, or more correctly Kingston upon Hull, is sited on low-lying land where the River Hull joins the broad Humber estuary, some 20 miles from the North Sea. It was this commercially and strategically important position that led to the foundation here of a port by the late 12th century when it was recorded as a leading centre for the export of wool. Known as Wyke upon Hull, the settlement then belonged to the wealthy Cistercian monastery of Meaux, some 6 miles north.

At some point in the mid 13th century the River Hull was re-aligned to its present position and the port moved eastward. In 1293 it was acquired by King Edward I who renamed the settlement Kingston, granted it a borough charter and planned a new town soon to be defended by high brick walls.

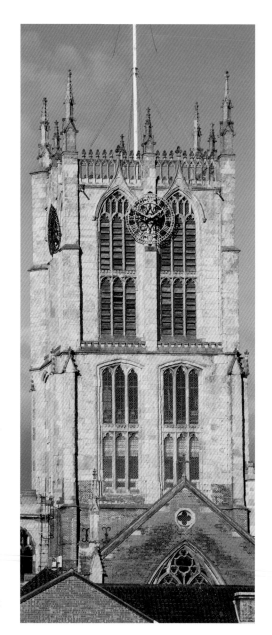

With access to Yorkshire and the Midlands via the rivers Ouse and Trent, and its location in relation to the Low Countries and the Baltic, Hull quickly became one of England's principal ports, a position it has retained to the present day. Few other English cities have ranked so high as centres of population and economic activity for more than seven centuries.

This long heritage has given Hull a wealth of historic buildings and places through which the city's proud story can be explored. It is a remarkable feature of Hull that it has retained so much of its medieval form, not only in the street pattern of the Old Town but also in the clear definition of its 14th-century boundary through the building of the Georgian docks along the line of the medieval walls. In no other great industrial or port city is the historic core so well defined.

Following the demolition of the town walls in the late 18th and early 19th century the built-up area spread rapidly north and west and the docks, originally located on the edge, were soon at the heart of the town. Today ships no longer sail through the city. But the presence of Humber and Railway Docks, retained as a marina, the former Prince's Dock and Queen's Gardens, site of the oldest dock, give Hull's centre a distinctive maritime flavour. This is enhanced by the wide Humber estuary and the River Hull that form the southern and eastern boundaries of the Old Town.

**Left:** View of Hull Minster from the Fruit Market.

**Below:** View across Hull Marina to Humber Dock Street and the Hessle Gate Buildings, a former rope factory that would have supplied thousands of ships on the Humber Estuary. During public realm improvements for UK City of Culture 2017, railway lines were uncovered on Humber Dock Street. They marked the shift from using riverboats to using locomotives to move cargo.

Although there are many historic buildings and places elsewhere in the city worthy of attention it is in the Old Town, the main focus of this booklet, where the long history of Hull can best be experienced. There are two medieval churches: Hull Minster (Holy Trinity Church) amongst the finest in England, built with the patronage of the Crown and leading merchants, and St Mary's. There is an Elizabethan former grammar school, where the merchants had their meeting place. Nearby is Trinity House, a great complex of Georgian buildings, which began as a medieval mariners' guild. On High Street are handsome examples of the merchants' homes of the 17th and 18th centuries, the older ones with a Dutch feel, reflecting the trading links that have made Hull a truly European city, independent but not isolated from the world.

# Medieval Hull: The Walled Town

In the 1290s, having conquered Wales, King Edward I turned his attention to establishing his authority in Scotland. With a military campaign imminent the king needed a supply port for his army and northern garrisons. Wyke upon Hull was ideal and Edward persuaded the monks of Meaux to swap the port for other property in 1293. He changed the name to Kingston (King's Town), and in 1299 granted the town borough status.

Although based on an existing settlement on the west bank of the River Hull, with houses already built along High Street that curves to follow the line of the river, Kingston was effectively a new town, one of a dozen founded by Edward I in England, Wales and Gascony. Much of the original layout is retained in the present street pattern of the Old Town, and its boundaries are still clearly identifiable, represented on the west and north by the Marina, Prince's Dock and Queen's Gardens, on the east by the river, and on the south by Humber Street.

The strategic and economic importance of Hull to the Crown, and its vulnerability, were affirmed in 1321 when King Edward II licensed the building of a ditch and wall. Between the late 1330s and 1410 some five million bricks were used to construct a high wall around three sides of the town. The River Hull ran along its east side. There were thirty interval towers and four main gates. The route of the walls and positions of towers and gates are marked in different colour bricks along the east side of Prince's Dock. The most important entrance was Beverley Gate guarding entry from Beverley and York (*see* page 11) The town walls defined and contained the town for four centuries, until they were demolished in the late 18th–early 19th centuries for the building of the first docks.

**Above:** 'Mortimer' is the life sized reconstruction of a Woolly Mammoth at the Hull and East Riding Museum.

VISIT **Hull & East Riding Museum of Archaeology, High Street.**
*Open daily, see:* http://www.hcandl.co.uk/museums

**Right:** Kingston upon Hull *c* 1540. The walls are shown with their gates and interval towers. The largest, Beverley Gate, is towards the top left-hand side with the road leading to the windmills. The River Humber is at the bottom. Ships are moored on the River Hull. On the east bank of the river is the village of Drypool. To the north outside the wall is Charterhouse. Within the walls are shown towards the bottom the tower of Hull Minster on the left and that of Blackfriars on the right. Further north to the middle left is the spire of the Carmelite Priory, towards the centre the tower of the de la Pole Manor House with the tower of St Mary's Church immediately to its right.

## City of Culture: **Made in Hull**

The bricks used to build the walls were made in Hull, which had the earliest documented brickworks in England. One was established by 1303 on the west side of the town, on a site now occupied by Prince's Dock, and another lay to the north at Trippet.

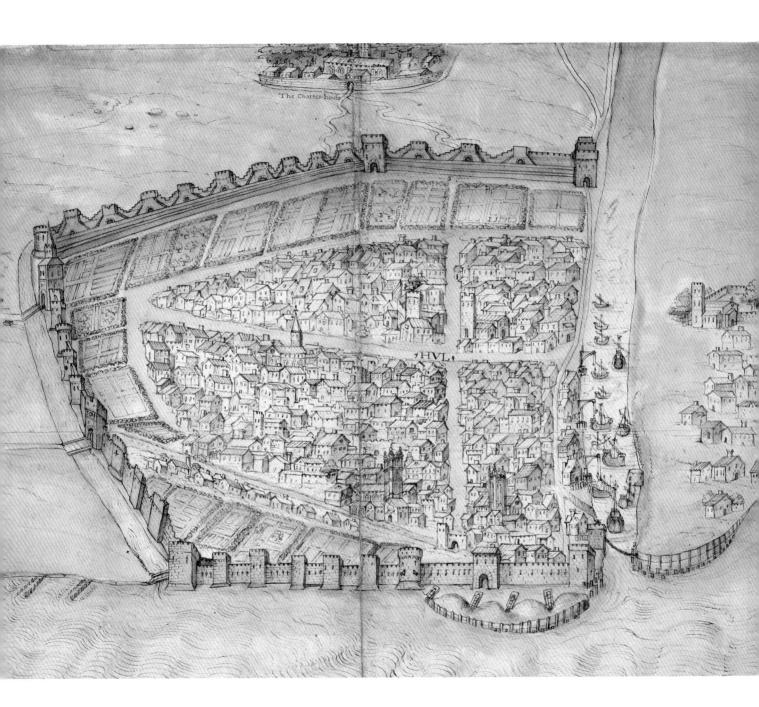

The Charter-house

HVL

5

# Medieval Hull: The Churches

The two fine medieval churches in the Old Town are rich treasure houses of the city's long history. Hull Minster, England's largest parish church by floor area, was built soon after the founding of Kingston upon Hull by Edward I, and royal masons were almost certainly involved. The earliest parts are the transepts and lower part of the tower built 1300–20, followed by the choir rebuilt 1340–70 and the nave 1380–1420.

Inside, the slender masonry structure and large windows give an impression of space and light. Fittings include an elaborate marble font of *c* 1380, late medieval bench ends and a stone pulpit with curving staircase from the 1840s restoration. The stained glass includes two fine windows by late-Victorian designer Walter Crane. The minster is packed with illuminating memorials to Hull's wealthy and influential inhabitants. Among them is an ornate mid 14th-century canopied tomb to a member of a leading merchant family, the de la Poles, a brass to Richard Byll who died 1451 of the plague, and a memorial to John Matthewson, died 1863, which mentions his role in securing a clean water supply for the townspeople.

King Edward I intended there to be only one church in Hull, but a second was built on land outside his control. Despite its tower dominating the north end of Lowgate, St Mary's Church is often overlooked. Said to be 'new built' in 1333 it was rebuilt from the later 14th century. The west end was destroyed when the tower collapsed in 1518. A new tower, built in brick in 1697, was encased in stone as part of the extensive restoration carried out in 1861–63 by Sir George Gilbert Scott who added a second south aisle to the nave. Most of the fittings are Victorian or later, including the carved screen of 1892 separating choir and nave.

Interesting monuments include a brass plate depicting a woollen draper who died in 1525, the bust of Alderman William Dobson, died 1666, and Georgian wall-tablets commemorating Benjamin Blaydes, shipbuilder, Joseph Pease, promoter of oil-seed crushing and founder of Hull's first bank, and Sir Samuel Standidge, who revived the whaling industry in the 1760s.

**Above:** Tower of St Mary's Church, Lowgate. Restored and enlarged by Sir George Gilbert Scott 1861-63 for his cousin, one of the three John Scotts, vicars of St Mary's, commemorated in the name of the pub opposite.

**Right:** Hull Minster to the east of the revamped Trinity Square, before the installation of the mirror pools.

## Medieval Hull: The Merchants and their Homes

The medieval prosperity of Hull was based upon the export of wool to the Continent, much of it coming from the great monasteries of Yorkshire and Lincolnshire. From the mid 14th century cloth and lead became the principal exports. The main imports were timber, corn and flax from the ports on the Baltic Sea, cod and herrings from Iceland, iron from Sweden and wine from Bordeaux in Gascony (part of France then held by the English kings). Hull was at one time second only to London in the wine trade, and one of the top three English ports for the export of wool and cloth, much of it to the Low Countries (now Holland and Belgium) and Baltic ports in the Hanseatic League such as Danzig (Poland) and Lubeck (Germany).

The de la Poles were financially, politically and socially the most successful of the merchant families in the new town of Hull. Their initial wealth was made through trade but their real fortune was made by large-scale money lending, particularly the vast sums lent by William de la Pole to Edward III to meet the costs of his Scottish campaigns. William's son Michael, who became 1st Earl of Suffolk and Chancellor to Richard II, rebuilt the large manor house that stood to the west of St Mary's Church (the 'Suffolk Palace') and three other houses, each with a tall tower and all of brick (now lost).

Many of the other medieval houses were timber-framed, including three substantial buildings that survived into the early 20th century on High Street, the favoured location for the merchants who wished to be close to their warehouses and staiths or private wharfs on the River Hull. Some were quite ornate, with decorative carved brackets and figures, as grand as anything to be found in York. The only surviving timber-framed house in Hull is no. 5 Scale Lane, probably built in the 15th century, although some timber building elements can be seen at the Hull and East Riding Museum.

**Above:** A medieval merchant and his wife, Hull Minster, south choir aisle. Probably Robert Selby and his wife Emma. Late 14th-century. Traditionally said to commemorate a member of the de la Pole family.

**Right:** The King's Head Inn, High Street, demolished in 1905.

# 16th and 17th Centuries: Port and Garrison

Hull suffered a decline in trade in the late 15th century, and it was not until a century later that its economy revived. One sign of growing prosperity was the building of the grammar school and merchants' exchange in the shadow of Hull Minster in 1583–5.

Earlier in the 16th century Hull had become an important military base. Following a visit in 1541 Henry VIII ordered defences to be built on the unprotected east side of the River Hull, as part of his scheme of fortifying the English coast. The new works consisted of three forts or blockhouses linked by a brick wall, the central one known as Hull Castle.

The castle became one of the two principal stores of arms and ammunition in England, giving Hull a key role in the build-up to the English Civil War. Wanting to secure the arms for his own use, Charles I tried to enter the town on 23 April 1642 but was turned away at Beverley Gate by the Governor,

**Above:** The Panelled 'Plotting Chamber' in the Olde White Harte Inn, 25 Silver Street.

**Left:** The Old Grammar School. This late 16th century early brick building had a large schoolroom on the ground floor, and merchants' exchange above. William Wilberforce and the poet Andrew Marvell were pupils here.

VISIT **Hands on History Museum, Old Grammar School, South Church Side.**
*Public access 12 noon-4pm on 2nd and 4th Saturday of each month, see: www.hcandl. co.uk/museums.*

## Beverley Gate

Beverley Gate *c* 1770 by Benjamin Gale

Part of the medieval brick gateway and a section of the adjoining wall were excavated in 1986–7. These remains, in a prominent location at the west end of Whitefriargate, were scheduled as an ancient monument by Historic England in 2016. Beverley Gate had an important role in the history of Hull.

Sir John Hotham, who had been appointed by Parliament. Following another failed attempt in July the town was besieged by Royalist forces for three weeks with another longer siege in September–October 1643. But it remained in Parliamentarian hands throughout the war.

In the 1680s the defences on the east side of the River Hull were reconstructed and the castle and south blockhouse incorporated into the Citadel, a triangular fort covering 30 acres. It was demolished in the 1860s.

The town again demonstrated its opposition to a Stuart king when the Catholic governor was overthrown following the landing of William of Orange (William III) in 1688. This action was planned at the Olde White Harte Inn, tucked away down a narrow passage off Silver Street, in a panelled room still known as the 'Plotting Chamber'. A gilded statue of William III on horseback, popularly known as King Billy, stands in Market Place.

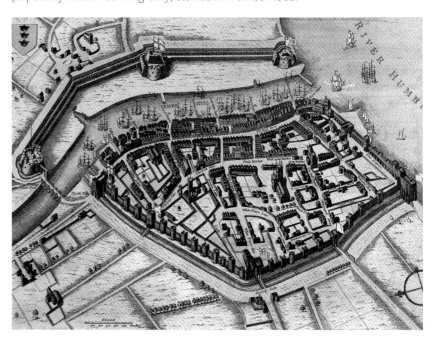

**Right:** Wenceslaus Hollar's plan of Hull *c* 1640 showing Henry VIII's defences at the top.

# 17th Century: The Dutch Connection

In the 17th century Hull had the appearance of a Dutch town, with brick town walls and gateways, surrounding water and steep-gabled houses along the river. Contact with Holland, particularly Amsterdam, was increasing at that time and Hull merchants were exposed to many influences from a country that then dominated world trade and much of the intellectual and cultural life of Western Europe.

Around 1660 Hugh Lister, who as a young man had been sent to Holland to gain trading experience, built himself a house on High Street that shows Dutch influence. Lister's house, now Wilberforce House has a very distinctive decorative brick facade with stone detailing and a projecting porch.

Soon the style was copied by others including the wealthy merchant George Crowle who in 1664 gave his house a new entrance front, now hidden away at the rear of 41 High Street, which echoes the porch of Wilberforce House. The architect of both houses was almost certainly the Hull bricklayer William Catlyn who was also responsible for the Olde White Harte, (see page 10) and buildings in a similar style in Lincolnshire. Some of the buildings had so-called Dutch or shaped gables of which one example survives at Charterhouse.

The major exports from Hull to Holland were corn and cloth manufactured in the West Riding, but the incoming cargoes were more varied including exotic goods such as East Indian spices, and iron pots and pans, pantiles, bricks, Delft tiles and the black marble gravestones found in large numbers in Hull Minster and other local churches. Pantiles, the curved roofing tiles, and the small yellow flooring bricks, 'clinkers', used for hearths and paths, were probably carried as ballast.

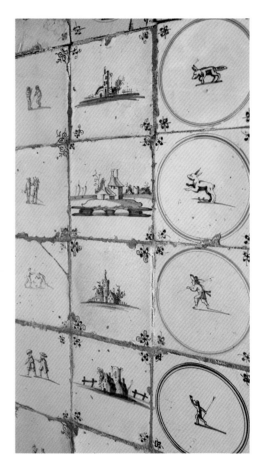

**Above:** Delft tiles from one of the fireplaces in Wilberforce House.

**Right:** William Wilberforce, anti-slave trade campaigner, was born in this fine 17th-century house in 1759.

VISIT **Wilberforce House (Museum of Slavery and Emancipation), High Street.**
*Open daily, see:* www.hcandl.co.uk/museums

# Georgian Hull: Merchants' Houses

From the mid-18th century Hull became Britain's fastest growing port, exporting the products of the industrial revolution from the mills and factories of West Yorkshire, Lancashire and the Midlands and importing the essential raw materials for the expanding industries: timber, iron, tar, hemp, flax and yarn from Scandinavia and the eastern Baltic (Russia, Poland and Germany).

The merchant families who became rich from this trade initially continued to live amongst the noise and smells of High Street, with their homes close to or adjoining their warehouses and private wharves on the River Hull. This arrangement can still be seen at Wilberforce House with its grounds running down to the river (*see* page 11).

The home of Henry Maister, who traded in iron and timber, on the west side of High Street was destroyed by fire in 1743 with the loss of his wife, a child and two maids. The following year work began on a new house on the site with advice from Lord Burlington, architect and great patron of the arts, a close acquaintance of Maister. The chief glory of Maister House, now owned by the National Trust, is the exquisite staircase, possibly designed by William Kent, the Bridlington-born architect, landscape garden and furniture designer. There are spectacular views up the stairwell to the glazed roof lantern.

The plasterwork at Maister House is by Joseph Page who is described on his gravestone as 'architect and master builder, of an extensive genius in the liberal arts; superior to many and excelled by few'. He probably designed Blaydes House, on 'Little' High Street when it was rebuilt *c* 1750 for Benjamin Blaydes. The Blaydes family were merchants and the port's leading shipbuilders; one of their former yards, now a disused dry dock, lies north of Blaydes House. Their most famous ship was the Bethia, built in 1782, which later became HMS Bounty of mutiny fame.

**Above:** Staircase at Maister House, High Street.

**Above:** Prince Street. In the early 1770s Joseph Page laid out King Street at the west end of Hull Minster with an archway leading through into the picturesque curving Prince Street.

## City of Culture: **Freedom**

William Wilberforce, the famous campaigner against the slave trade, was born in High Street, Hull in 1759. A member of a wealthy merchant family he recalled how 'the theatre, balls, great suppers, and card-parties were the delight of the principal families in the town'. His birthplace, Wilberforce House, is now a museum that tells the story of the trans-Atlantic slave trade and its abolition (*see* page 13). Hull was not involved in the slave trade. The city is twinned with Freetown, Sierra Leone.

William Wilberforce by Karl Hickel, 1794

On High Street, south of Alfred Gelder Street, is the site of the home of Joseph Pease, an18th-century merchant who was born in Holland. He traded in oil seeds, such as rape and hemp, established his own seed crushing mill, developed other commercial interests such as paint making and cotton spinning, and in 1754 founded Hull's first bank. Although his house was demolished after the war, a remarkable survival is the long range of four-storey brick and pantile warehouses behind bearing his initials. Dated 1745 and 1760, they face the River Hull, and were successfully converted into flats in the early 1980s.

# Georgian Hull: The First Dock, New Town and Charterhouse

As the 18th century progressed the number of ships entering and leaving the port rose each year, and the River Hull became congested, particularly with the development of the whaling trade. The customs officers found it difficult to check goods as this had to be done either on board or on the merchants' private staiths. It was proposed that a dock be built, to relieve pressure on the river, and provide a 'legal quay' for customs purposes.

In 1774 the Hull Dock Company was set up, and New, later Queen's Dock was opened four years later. Covering about 11 acres, it was the largest inland dock in Britain when built. Last used in 1930, it was filled in and Queen's Gardens laid out.

A few years after the dock was opened Parliament Street (which runs north from Whitefriargate towards Queen's Gardens) was formed, providing a route from the Old Town to the dock. The most complete street of Georgian houses in the city, it has long been the haunt of solicitors and accountants.

To build the dock part of the medieval town wall had to be demolished. This released land to the north, and Hull began to expand. The 'new town' or Northern Suburb north of the dock had 'many very handsome, well-built houses' to which several merchants relocated from High Street.

**Left:** East view of the bridge and the new dock at Kingston upon Hull, painting by Robert Thew, 1786.

**Above:** The merchant Joseph R. Pease's eleven-bay mansion was the finest in an impressive terrace of fifteen large houses that stood on Charlotte Street, now part of George Street, of which only two remain (nos. 83–5) built *c* 1782.

**Far right:** Charterhouse, entrance front, Charterhouse Lane.

## St Charles Borromeo

In 1828–9 a Roman Catholic church, St Charles Borromeo, was built in Jarratt Street in the Northern Suburb. Alterations in the 1830s and 1890s gave the church its dramatic Baroque interior.

Beyond the Northern Suburb lies Charterhouse, a splendid late 18th-century almshouse building on Charterhouse Lane, just west of the industrial area called Wincolmlee which runs parallel to the River Hull. It was founded on this site, outside the walled town, by the Hull merchant William de la Pole in 1354, and later in the 14th century the de la Poles established a Carthusian priory alongside. That was destroyed at the Reformation but the almshouse survived.

The hospital was demolished in 1643 prior to the second siege of Hull during the Civil War to prevent its occupation by the Royalists. It was rebuilt a few years later, then replaced by the present structure in 1778–80, designed by a local architect, Joseph Hargrave. Inside is a delightful unspoilt Georgian chapel, complete with box pews.

The Master's House, opposite, with a large garden behind, dates from the 17th and 18th centuries although it was heavily restored in the 1950s after severe war damage. Andrew Marvell (1621–78), poet and MP for Hull, was a son of a Master of Charterhouse and spent much of his childhood in a house on this site.

# Georgian Hull: Docks and the Waterfront

By the end of the 18th century the first dock was overcrowded and in 1809 a second, this time entered directly from the Humber, was opened. Humber Dock and its mid 19th-century extension, Railway Dock, became a marina in 1983, and here there is still an impression of what the area must have been like when it was the hub of the busy port. The quayside at the entrance is where the packet steamers berthed in the later 19th century, bringing many transmigrants from The Baltic and Scandinavia.

Most of the imposing brick warehouses that lined the dock sides have gone but one on the south side of Railway Dock, No. 13, seven storeys high, has been kept. On the east side of Humber Dock stands the old Humber Dock Tavern, with its green glazed bricks and decorative panels added in 1907. The Spurn Lightship, a navigation aid for ships entering the Humber estuary, and now a museum, is moored at the Marina.

**Below:** The Steam Packet Wharf located within the Humber Dock Basin was used by some of the earliest steam-powered ships plying the route between Europe and Hull.

The building of the docks had a big impact on Hull. The last section of the medieval town wall was demolished when Prince's (originally Junction) Dock was built in 1829 to link Queen's and Humber Dock, so the Old Town became almost an island, surrounded by water on all sides.

The excavated soil from Humber Dock was used to reclaim land from the estuary; everything that lies to the south of Humber Street was previously under water. Once a flourishing close-built area of houses, merchants' offices, pubs, a chapel, a theatre, and until recently a thriving wholesale fruit market, it is now undergoing major regeneration. To the south is Nelson Street, a quiet, unchanged area alongside the Humber, which retains some attractive buildings including the handsome former Pilot Office built in 1819–20 - the pilots guided ships along the Humber. At the opposite end of Nelson Street, at the end of Minerva Terrace, stands the three-storey Minerva Hotel, built a few years later on a triangular plot, which accounts for its unusual shape. In between later buildings include the former booking offices for the Humber ferry, which sailed from Victoria Pier, connecting Hull with New Holland in Lincolnshire, until the opening of the Humber Bridge in 1981.

This is a popular place from which to admire the Humber and a convenient place to use the rather impressive Edwardian style public toilets. A welcome addition to the scene has been The Deep aquarium (*see* pages 43–44) which rises majestically over the estuary. It stands on the opposite bank of the River Hull, and the view to the Old Town is framed by the Tidal Surge Barrier, built in 1980.

**Above:** Former Pilot Office, Queen Street.

**Left:** Victoria Pier Edwardian style toilets on Nelson Street.  Known for having potted plants inside the building to complement the white tiles and copper pipes interior, these toilets have even been listed in visitor guides.

# Georgian Hull: Trinity House

Some of the Old Town's finest buildings are those erected in the Georgian period on the Trinity House estate that covers all the land between Posterngate and Whitefriargate. Trinity House was established in the Middle Ages to look after the interests of the town's maritime community, providing support for poor seamen and their families, regulating wages and working conditions, and later taking control of shipping and navigation on the Humber.

In the early 14th century a Carmelite friary was built on this site. Whitefriargate takes its name from the friars, who wore white cloaks. Part of the land was leased to Trinity House, and a guildhall, chapel and almshouses were built there. In 1621 Thomas Ferres, a wealthy shipmaster, gave the site to Trinity House.

The earliest surviving buildings stand on the corner of Trinity House Lane and Posterngate, and are grouped around a courtyard, although this is not obvious from the street. Some parts are probably medieval, but what are visible are two sides of a range of almshouses, built 1753–9. Over the main entrance, on Trinity House Lane, is an elaborate and colourful pediment with a richly carved coat of arms, flanked by the reclining figures of Neptune, God of the Sea, and Britannia.

Moving west along Posterngate, Carmelite House was built in 1826 as the Trinity Almshouses, and behind lies a chapel of 1839 that can be seen by entering the gateway into Zebedee's Yard. Nearby is the Ferres Hospital which provided more accommodation for retired seamen and their widows.

The site fronting Whitefriargate provided Trinity House with an opportunity to make money from commercial development through the building of some of Hull's finest Georgian architecture. Most impressive is nos. 11–14 (Boot's and adjoining property), built 1794–5 as the Neptune Inn (Neptune's head adorns the ground-floor archway). The large Venetian window on the first floor lights the banqueting room which retains a decorative plaster ceiling. Almost as splendid if more restrained is Smith's bank, the central portion of a larger block (nos. 1–9) of 1829–30. The pediment has the usual nautical theme, a permanent reminder that it was built by the 'House'.

**Right:** The main entrance of Trinity House, 1758–9.

VISIT **Trinity House, Trinity House Lane.**
*Trinity House is open for guided tours on selected days of the year. For information on upcoming tours, please visit:* www.hullboxoffice.com/events/hull-trinity-house-tour
*For further information on Hull Trinity House see:* http://www.trinityhousehull.org.uk/

# Victorian Hull: The Coming of the Railway

Hull's continued prosperity at the beginning of the 19th century was in part due to its links via the Humber, Ouse and Trent rivers to a network of inland waterways used to carry goods for export from the heavily industrialised towns of West Yorkshire and much of the Midlands. This gave the port an advantage which was threatened when the first railways were built in the region, providing a viable alternative to water transport.

A line from Leeds to Selby was opened in 1834 but it was not until 1840 that it was extended to Hull, providing the town with a rail link to the West Riding. The first station, a modest affair, was close to Humber Dock. Following the opening of a branch line to Bridlington in 1846 the larger Paragon Station (named after Paragon Street) was built in a more central location. Designed by the notable railway architect G.T. Andrews, it opened in 1848.

The building faces Anlaby Road, although this is no longer the main entrance. The central block, two storeys high, was the original booking hall. Andrews also designed the adjoining Station Hotel (now the Royal Hotel). In 1903–4 William Bell, then architect to the North Eastern Railway, extended the station, making a new entrance on the east side facing what would later become Ferensway.

Bell was responsible for the impressive five-span station platform roof (best viewed from the Park Street bridge), and also designed a new booking hall with a pleasing tiled interior and central wooden ticket office.

**Above:** Opened in 1848, this was the original booking hall and entrance to Paragon Station, to the north of Anlaby Road.

**Far left:** Paragon Station roof from Park Street.

**Right:** Former Emigrant Waiting Room, Anlaby Road that would have seen many of the 2.2 million emigrants who passed through the platform at Hull Train Station as they headed west.

# Victorian Hull: The Maritime Museum

Between the opening of the railway in 1840 and the end of the century the population of Hull rose from around 65,000 to 240,000. The docks, fishing, shipbuilding and processing industries such as seed crushing and paint manufacture, which depended on imported linseed, provided the main employment. Ship-owners and industrialists rather than gentleman merchants dominated the society of the port. These included men such as Charles Wilson (later Lord Nunburnholme) and his brother Arthur who in the 1860s took over what became the largest independent steamship company in the world, the Wilson Line.

A great increase in trade and the growing size of ships required the building of new docks along the Humber in the second half of the 19th century, and the work of the Hull Dock Company, based in a Georgian building close to the river, expanded. Larger and centrally-placed premises were needed, and the company decided to commission a new, more prestigious building. A competition held in 1866 to design the new Dock Offices was won by a London-based architect, Christopher George Wray. His design was an imaginative one, well suited to take advantage of the restricted site on an island of land between Queen's Dock and Prince's Dock. The building was completed in 1871, some thirty years before Queen Victoria Square was laid out. Three distinctive domes dominate the skyline.

One of the great joys of the building, both inside and out, is the wealth of detail in the sculpture and other decorative work, incorporating maritime symbols including dolphins, mermaids, scallop shells and starfish. Especially delightful are the surrounding railings, topped with gilded tridents (three-pronged spears), a symbol of the sea-god Neptune decorated with delicate little dolphin heads. Inside the building a wide stone staircase with wrought-iron balustrade leads to the first floor and the grand Court Room, the meeting place for the company's shareholders.

**Above:** A sculpture of Neptune and his wife Amphitrite riding seahorses flanking the arms used by the Hull Dock Company (the 18th-century Royal Arms).

**Right:** The Maritime Museum (former Town Dock Offices). In 1975 the Dock Offices were converted to a fascinating museum devoted to Hull's maritime history, including displays about whaling and deep-sea fishing.

VISIT **The Maritime Museum, Queen Victoria Square.**
*Open daily, see:* http://www.hcandl.co.uk/museums

# Victorian Hull: Maritime Heritage

## The Eastern Docks

One of the city's most successful modern housing developments is Victoria Dock village, on the east bank of the River Hull, facing the Humber estuary. It is built on the site of the first of the eastern docks, and close to where the 17th-century fort known as the Citadel once stood (*see* page 11). Opened in 1850, Victoria Dock was built to serve the timber trade and had entrances from both river and estuary. In 1863 it was extended to cover some 25 acres. In 1970 the dock was closed. It was filled in, and from 1989 onwards the 'village' was built. Its character is helped by the retention of the impressive stone-lined Half-Tide Basin, the name given to the inner section of the entrance to Victoria Dock from the Humber. Apartments have been built overlooking the water.

Another water feature is the former slipway. At the north end stands the Winding House, which had a steam-powered winch to haul vessels ashore for repair. A great attraction is the promenade along the Humber estuary opened in 1992 that links into a public footpath making it possible to walk east from The Deep past Victoria Dock village to the later docks. The first of these, Alexandra Dock, still in use, was built 1880–5 for exporting coal, the next - King George Dock - opened in 1914 and the last - Queen Elizabeth Dock - in 1969.

**Above:** The Fish trail.

FOLLOW the Fish Trail around the Old Town. The 41 pieces of pavement sculpture by Gordon Young all depict life-size fish.
*Leaflet available from Tourist Information Centre.*

**Left:** Victoria Dock Village, Victoria Dock, Half-Tide Basin.

Above: The Arctic Corsair.

VISIT The Arctic Corsair, Hull's last surviving sidewinder trawler, berthed on the River Hull behind Streetlife Museum. The Arctic Corsair is moving in early 2019 to accommodate Environment Agency flood defence works on the River Hull.
*To book guided tours, and for information on when the vessel will be moved, please see:*
https://www.hcandl.co.uk/museums

Right: Former Winding House (before conversion to flats), Victoria Dock. It contained a steam-powered winch to haul vessels up the slipway for repair.

## The Western Docks and the Fishing Industry

In the 18th and early 19th centuries Hull was a whaling port, but trawl fishing did not begin until the 1840s. The first trawlers came from Devon and Kent, attracted by the discovery of the Silver Pits fishing ground, 30 miles east of Spurn Point. At first the fishermen lived near Humber Dock, where their vessels tied up, but in 1869 Albert Dock, the first of the western docks, was built and Hessle Road became the heart of the fishing community. A decade later some 7,000 fishing voyages were being made annually from the port.

In 1883 St Andrew's Dock was opened specifically as a fish dock, with a fish market (Billingsgate) on the dockside. By this date the nature of the fishing industry was changing, as the old wooden smacks began to be replaced by much larger steam trawlers. Another development was the growth of the fish curing industry, and a handful of distinctive smoke houses survive in the area.

Deep-sea fishing more or less ended in the 1970s. St Andrew's Dock was closed and later largely filled in. A retail park now covers much of the site.

## Victorian and Edwardian Hull: Shops and Pubs

As a major retail centre Hull served not only much of the East Riding but also the residents of north Lincolnshire, who regularly crossed the Humber by ferry or market boat. For local residents a network of trams as well as omnibus services provided transport to the city centre.

Hull has two shopping arcades. The earlier and more modest is Paragon Arcade, 1892 by W. A. Gelder, which runs from Paragon Street to Carr Lane, and has a fine decorative cast-iron and glazed roof. More impressive is Hepworth's arcade by Gelder & Kitchen, 1894–5, built for a Leeds tailor, Joseph Hepworth. L-shaped, it links Market Place and Silver Street and when first built had 26 shop units, including a Marks & Spencer 'Penny Bazaar'. The elegant two-storey interior has decorative pilasters and a glazed barrel-vaulted roof with an octagonal dome. There is access from the arcade into the imposing Edwardian Market Hall that lies to the north of Hull Minster.

The city has a fine collection of pubs. Among the most decorative is the Punch Hotel in Queen Victoria Square. Built in 1896 it has a 'fairy-tale' facade of red brick with elaborate shaped gables, ornate bay windows, and much terracotta detail. In the Old Town there are several pubs with good interiors, notably the Olde Black Boy, High Street, the Olde Blue Bell, Market Place, and the Olde White Harte, Silver Street.

**Above:** The Punch Hotel, Queen Victoria Square.

**Left:** Streetlife Museum.

VISIT **Streetlife Museum, High Street.**
This fascinating purpose-built museum, which primarily tells the story of transport in Hull, has a streetscene gallery with several period reconstructed shops.
*Open daily, see:* http://www.hcandl.co.uk/museums

**Above:** Opened in 1806 as New Dock Tavern, the public house was re-named Humber Dock Tavern in 1839. Until recently, it was known as The Green Bricks, after the distinctive green glazed exterior brickwork.

**Right:** Papier maché and muslin elephants in Hepworth's Arcade being filmed as part of the bid to be UK City of Culture 2017. They formed part of the programme as there used to be elephants in large zoological gardens on Spring Bank, Hull. They would walk through the town to be washed in the River Hull.

# Edwardian Hull: City Hall

Hull was at the peak of its prosperity in the years between the death of Queen Victoria and the First World War. It was the third port in Britain after London and Liverpool in the value of trade, it was the country's leading fishing port and its industries were booming. This prosperity, and pride in the city status granted in 1897, is evidenced by the scale and quality of the many buildings that survive from these years.

It was through the initiative of the architect William Alfred Gelder, Mayor 1899–1903, that the centre of the city was transformed and grand civic buildings erected. The close-built area of shops, offices and tenement buildings that hemmed in the handsome Dock Offices (Maritime Museum) were cleared away and Queen Victoria Square created. A bronze statue of the late Queen was placed in the centre, and on the west side the imposing domed City Hall was built 1903–10.

A venue for entertainment, public meetings and civic events with art gallery attached, the City Hall was designed in an Edwardian Baroque-style by Joseph H. Hirst, who had been appointed the first City Architect in 1900. Portraits of great artists and other scenes decorate the exterior of the building which has shops to the ground floor.

Buildings by Joseph Hirst are dotted all over the city and include the Beverley Road Baths, the handsome Market Hall alongside Hull Minster, grand Neo-Georgian schools, Tudor almshouses, and Arts and Crafts-style lodges at cemeteries and parks. Most charming of all is the half-timbered former Carnegie Library, 1905, at the gates of West Park on Anlaby Road.

Hirst contributed more than any other architect to the landscape of the proud Edwardian city but he was not chosen to design its grandest building, the new Guildhall and Law Courts.

**Above:** The staircase inside City Hall.

**Right:** City Hall in the background. In the foreground, the 250 foot long wind turbine blade installed in Queen Victoria Square as part of the 2017 Made In Hull season.

# Edwardian Hull: Guildhall and Law Courts

No sooner had work begun on the City Hall than a competition was held to select an architect for the rebuilding of the cramped court rooms at the rear of the Town Hall, which dated from 1862–5, and the provision of a new council chamber and offices.

The competition was won by a young Edwin Cooper, an important Edwardian architect, originally from Scarborough. The vast building he designed, erected 1905–11, stretches for thirty-five bays along the north side of Alfred Gelder Street, a wide road that recently had been cut through a maze of slum housing at the northern edge of the Old Town.

The south facade of this major civic building, like so many of the period, is in a bold English Baroque style of the early 18th century. Fifteen-bay colonnades of giant Composite columns flank a massive three-bay entrance block with large pavilions at either end. The latter are topped by colossal sculptures of the 'Daughters of Neptune'.

Just as the work was in its final stages the architect persuaded the City Council to replace the fifty-year old Town Hall with a building to his design more in keeping with the new courts. Begun in 1913, and completed in the middle of the First World War, the Guildhall is plainer in style. Inside there is a vast banqueting room running the whole width of the building and a smaller cube-shaped and domed reception room, but what impresses are the long dark panelled corridors and the magnificent domed council chamber. The bench ends are suitably carved with maritime themes. Mounted on top of the Grade II* listed Guildhall clock tower is a timeball with a mast held in place by four stone putti (similar in appearance to cherubs). The ball was raised so that it would drop at a precise moment, normally 12 noon, to notify ships in the harbour and estuary of the exact time. Such visible signals were vital for accurate navigation, although by the time the Hull timeball was erected telegraphy was mostly in use at England's major ports. The mechanism has not worked for a long time and will be restored in 2019 using a Heritage Grant from the National Lottery.

**Above:** The Council Chamber ceiling in the Guildhall adorned with plasterwork white roses.

**Above:** View from Bourne Street with Wilberforce Monument, the tower of St Mary's Church and the Guildhall. On the top of the Guildhall is the timeball.

**Left:** Spencer Tunick's Sea of Hull installation on Alfred Gelder Street with the Guildhall in the background.

# Hull: The Bombed City

Hull was bombed several times by Zeppelin airships during the First World War, and a number of civilians were killed and houses destroyed.

During the Second World War Hull suffered more bomb damage than any other urban area outside London. The docks were the main target but the destruction was spread throughout the city. There were 86 raids, the first on 20 June 1940 and the last on 17 March 1945, with the heaviest bombing in the spring and summer of 1941. In May that year, on two consecutive nights, hundreds of heavy explosive bombs and tens of thousands of incendiaries were dropped and at times the whole city seemed to be on fire. Everywhere houses, offices, shops, schools, churches, factories, mills and warehouses were ablaze and streets were blocked by fallen debris or cut into by large craters.

During the war some 1,200 people were killed in Hull and 152,000 made homeless. Of the city's 92,600 houses fewer than 6,000 were undamaged. In the city centre half the principal shops were lost as well as six cinemas and two theatres. Whole streets were razed to the ground and many historic buildings were destroyed or severely damaged, and subsequently demolished. These included over 30 churches, chapels and synagogues and the Royal Institution on Albion Street, one of the city's finest buildings. The City Hall and the Guildhall did not escape damage but both continued in use, with the ornate council chamber being used as an emergency feeding centre.

A powerful reminder of the impact of the Second World War on the city is the facade of the former National Picture Theatre on Beverley Road. This cinema, built in 1914, was largely destroyed on the night of 18 March 1941. An audience of 150 was watching the Charlie Chaplin film 'The Great Dictator' when the air raid sirens sounded. They took shelter in the foyer and all survived when a bomb exploded near the screen. The cinema's shell has been designated a Grade II listed building, because of its national significance as a rare physical reminder of damage caused by wartime air raids.

Bomb-damaged buildings 1941.
**Top:** City Hall and Prudential Building, Queen Victora Square.
**Middle:** Georgian houses, High Street.
**Bottom:** Royal Institution, Albion Street.

**Above:** The former National Picture Theatre, Beverley Road.

Before the end of the war Hull Corporation commissioned a wide-ranging plan for the reconstruction of the city. Fortunately little of the ambitious 'Abercrombie Plan' was implemented for it would have destroyed the character of the Old Town.

In the city centre, rebuilding of the shops was underway by the late 1940s. The extensive neo-Georgian Queen's House between Jameson, King Edward and Paragon Streets of 1951–2 has worn well, as has the former Hammonds department store, 1950, on Ferensway.

## Amy Johnson, Pioneer Aviator

Born in Hull in 1903, Amy Johnson was the first female pilot to fly solo from Britain to Australia. During the Second World War she flew planes for the Air Transport Auxiliary. She died on 5 January 1941 when the plane she was flying crashed in the Thames estuary.

**Right:** An installation on Humber Dock Street for 'A Moth for Amy', a public art project to mark the 75th anniversary of Amy Johnson's death. Johnson flew a de Havilland Gipsy Moth to Australia as well as several other de Havilland Moths during her flying career.

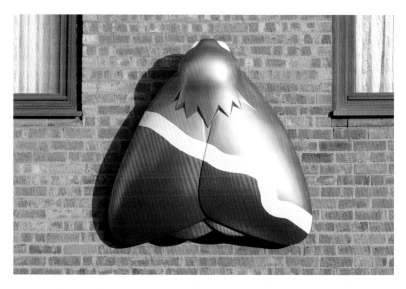

# Made in Hull: Entrepreneurs

In the 19th century several enterprising men in Hull established small businesses that would eventually become multinational companies. Among these was Joseph Rank, founder of Rank's flour millers, who began by renting a windmill on Holderness Road. His son, J. Arthur Rank, born in 1888, went on to found the Rank film organization. Another local entrepreneur was Thomas James Smith, a pharmaceutical chemist. With the help of his nephew Horatio he built up Smith & Nephew, makers of medical goods. High demand for surgical dressings during the First World War resulted in rapid expansion of the business.

One of Hull's major employers in the 20th century, Reckitt & Colman (now RB), manufacturers of iconic brands such as Brasso and Dettol, developed from a starch manufactory established by Isaac Reckitt in Dansom Lane in 1840. The city owes much to the philanthropy of Isaac's sons, Sir James Reckitt, and that of Thomas R. Ferens, one of the company's directors. Ferens provided the art gallery that bears his name as well as the site that is now the University of Hull together with a substantial donation.

## Garden Village

In 1907 Sir James Reckitt, a Quaker, purchased the 130-acre Holderness House estate, on Holderness Road, in order to build better houses, in a pleasant setting, for his workforce. The following year Garden Village, an attractive suburb with tree-lined streets, designed by Hull architects Runton & Barry, was officially opened.

The Oval, Garden Village: A pair of 'first-class' houses designed for supervisory staff.

**Left:** Ferens Art Gallery by Cooke and Davies 1926-7.

Founded as a University College, the earliest buildings (now named Cohen and Venn, the latter in tribute to Hull-born mathematician John Venn) on the original (East) Cottingham Road campus are by William A. Forsyth, 1928. In 1954 full university status was granted, and the present campus layout owes much to the vision of Leslie Martin who was appointed consultant architect in 1958. Noteworthy buildings include the Middleton Hall and Larkin Building, 1965–7, to Martin's own designs, the Sports and Fitness Centre (most recently listed in December 2016), 1963–5 by Peter Womersley and the Gulbenkian Centre (an innovative drama teaching centre), 1969–70 by Peter Moro & Partners. Major additions were made 1966–9 to the University library, described by its Librarian Philip Larkin (*see* page 38) as a 'lifted study-storehouse'. This building was recently modernised.In 2002 the University expanded into the neighbouring (West) campus, where the buildings include four original blocks of a teacher training college established in 1913. Recently, the University has worked with Historic England to modernise the offer for students involving the expansion and remodelling of The Middleton Hall.

**Above:** Bas-relief sculpture of an owl, by Willi Soukop, on the exterior of the Brynmor Jones Library. Sir Brynmor Jones initiated the research in the field of Liquid Crystals (LCD) at Hull University.

**Right:** Middleton Hall (before remodelling), 1965-7, by Leslie Martin.

## Liquid Crystal Displays

In 1973 a team of chemists at the University of Hull, led by Dr (later Professor) George Gray, made the major scientific breakthrough that allows displays to be made from liquid crystals.

# City of Culture

Hull is justifiably proud of its legacy as UK City of Culture in 2017, a title awarded every four years to a place that demonstrates the belief in the transformational power of culture. The city can already claim many former residents who have made their mark in the arts.

Great names in the literary world include the Hull-born 17th-century metaphysical poet Andrew Marvell and 20th-century poet and novelist Philip Larkin, who was Librarian at the University from 1955 until his death in 1985. A statue of him stands in the foyer of Paragon Station. Other former University staff or students include Andrew Motion, Poet-Laureate 1999–2009, poets Douglas Dunn and Roger McGough, and the playwright Anthony Minghella. The poet Stevie Smith was born in the city.

In the field of art the 17th-century Dutch master Rembrandt is thought to have spent some time in Hull towards the end of his life, and a century later George Stubbs, most famous for his horse paintings, worked here as a portrait painter. Hull was the birthplace in 1869 of celebrated international art dealer (Sir) Jospeh Duveen, son of a Dutch-Sephardic Jewish immigrant. Several of his paintings were given to the Ferens Art Gallery in Queen Victoria Square (website **www. hcandl.co.uk/ferens**). Opened in 1927, it is one of the best provincial galleries in the country, with works by artists ranging from Frans Hals and Canaletto to David Hockney. John Ward of Hull, the best of the local Victorian maritime artists, is well-represented. The University of Hull has a public gallery with a small but outstanding collection of British Art 1890–1940 (website **https:// www.hull.ac.uk/choose-hull/study-at-hull/library/visitors/index.aspx**).

Several Hull-born actors have become household names, including Tom Courtenay, brought up in the heart of the Hessle Road fishing community, Maureen Lipman, and Ian Carmichael. The city is fortunate to have two major theatres. The New Theatre in Kingston Square, originally the Assembly Rooms, provides an ideal venue to see performances by leading theatre and dance companies. Outside stands a statue of singer David Whitfield, born in Hull in 1925. Hull Truck, which began as a small experimental back-street theatre in Spring Street in 1971, moved to its present state of the art building in Ferensway in 2009 when the St Stephen's shopping centre was built.

## The Fruit Market

Smoke House, Wellington Street.

The regeneration of the former wholesale Fruit Market in Humber Street, on land reclaimed from the estuary in the early 19th century, is rapidly turning this area into a vibrant cultural quarter. Located close to the busy Marina, it offers art galleries, restaurants, markets, live music and theatre.

**Above:** Hull Fair at the Fair Ground, Walton Street taken on 10 October 1952. An annual fair has been held in Hull since medieval times. Trade in goods and animals dominated the early fairs but, from the 18th century, entertainment became the most important aspect of the event.

**Right:** Statue of Philip Larkin by Martin Jennings, 2010, Paragon Station, Hull.
The poet is also commemorated by a literary trail around the city and further afield.
*see website:* www.thelarkintrail.co.uk

## City of Culture: Tell the World

Hull is proud of its cream telephone boxes, a legacy of the Corporation telephone system set up in 1902. Sale of shares by the City Council when the service was privatised in 1999 provided funds for the splendid KCOM Stadium, a sports venue which hosts major concerts and other events.

Alongside Hull Truck theatre is the striking blue cone-shaped Albermarle Music Centre, which has a performance area as well teaching and rehearsal rooms for local musical ensembles, and has played a key role in nurturing young talent. Music has always been important in the city, which has several orchestras and choirs including the Hull Philharmonic Orchestra which performs regularly in the City Hall (*see* page 30). This splendid venue has welcomed many visiting performers including members of the Royal Philharmonic Orchestra who have worked in partnership with local musicians.

Hull-born musicians include the concert pianist Ethel Leginska who was also one of the earliest female conductors, folk singers The Watersons, and guitarist Mick Ronson who played alongside David Bowie. The popular Housemartins were a Hull band.

Highlights of the city's annual calendar include the hugely popular Freedom Festival incorporating many aspects of culture ranging from music and dance to art and comedy. A great family tradition among local residents is a visit to the week-long October fun fair, one of Europe's largest travelling fairs, which takes place in Walton Street. Sport too plays a big role in the city's popular culture, the two professional Rugby League teams, Hull F.C. and Hull Kingston Rovers, and football team, Hull City, having thousands of loyal supporters.

Hull's winning bid to become UK City of Culture 2017 proclaimed 'This City belongs to Everyone'. Building upon the events held during 2017, Absolutely Cultured are delivering a legacy programme focusing on the unique character of the city, its people, history and geography to cement the long-term future of Hull as a cultural destination.

**Immediate left:** Explore the KCOM phone box trail, starting in Trinity Market at the Grade II listed K1 phone box.
*see website:* https://www.kcomhome.com/campaigns/trail/

**Far left:** Humber Street in the Fruit Market undergoing major regeneration.

# Regeneration - Humber Bridge to Green Port

The regeneration of the city following the virtual end of the fishing industry and a decline in manufacturing in the 1970s has continued to draw on the city's maritime heritage. The opening of the Humber Bridge to the west of the city in 1981 led to a greater appreciation of the Humber estuary and the lower stretch of the River Hull was enhanced by the great arch of the tidal surge barrier. This was followed by the conversion of two of the town docks to a lively marina and the imaginative development of the Princes Quay Shopping Centre within Prince's Dock. Further east, the housing development associated with the former Victoria Dock made the most of its position on the Humber.

**Below:** Stage@TheDock is an amphitheatre that cantilevers into the Grade II listed dry dock with the Centre for Digital Industries (C4DI) building to the rear.

**Above:** The Tidal Surge Barrier.

Hull began to reunite the city centre with its waterfronts along the Humber and River Hull with an emphasis on buildings of high architectural quality and originality. The city has a number of 21st-century buildings that have made positive additions to the townscape. Three highlights are the waterfront landmark of The Deep aquarium, 2002, by Terry Farrell and Partners; the distinctive One Humber Quays, 2005, by DLA Architecture; and the Hull History Centre, 2009, by Pringle Richards Sharratt with its cushion-roofed arcade.

The Hull City Plan, published in 2013, incorporates an ambitious and coordinated strategy to revitalise Hull, capitalising on the city's position at the heart of the UK's biggest port complex and its legacy as UK City of Culture 2017.

As part of the 'Energy City' ambition to be a world class centre for renewable energy it was decided, in 2012, to adapt the historic Alexandra Dock for a major investment in assembly of off-shore wind turbines known as Green Port Hull. To date, this development has created over 2,000 jobs in the renewable energy sector and its supply chain, providing a significant boost to Hull's economy.

The 'Destination Hull' elements of the City Plan are as varied as they are ambitious. New schemes of paving, landscaping and public art were delivered in preparation for Hull's year as UK City of Culture 2017. The redevelopment of the Fruit Market is well-advanced with the distinctive C4DI and Stage@The Dock development hosting work space for digital and technology companies as well as outdoor performance space in the Dry Dock. The city continues to build upon the regeneration work undertaken to date, with the installation of an iconic footbridge across the A63 to provide an easier route between the Fruit Market and the rest of the Old Town; the redevelopment of Albion Square and an international cruise terminal for Yorkshire.

# Further Reading

This booklet has been based on material gathered for *Hull* (Yale University Press, 2010) by David and Susan Neave, part of the prestigious 'Pevsner Architectural Guides' series. With colour photographs and maps, that publication is a more in-depth study of the city's history through its buildings. Detailed walks cover the suburbs as well as the central area principally dealt with here.

Buildings of the 18th and early 19th centuries are examined in Ivan and Elisabeth Hall's authoritative and well-illustrated *Georgian Hull* (1978) The period 1830–1914 is covered by *Architecture of the Victorian Era of Kingston upon Hull* by Ian N. Goldthorpe, ed. M. Sumner (2005). For historic pubs see David Gamston (ed.) *Yorkshire's Real Heritage Pubs* (2011). *Lost Churches and Chapels of Hull* (1991), by David Neave and others and five excellent volumes of *Hull Then and Now* by Paul Gibson (2008–15) record lost buildings and townscape. For coloured engravings and early views of buildings, monuments and street scenes of Hull, see also *An Historical Map of Kingston Upon Hull* eds D.H. Evans, David Neave and Susan Neave (2017).

The standard work on the history of Hull is K.J. Allison (ed.), *Victoria County History, Yorkshire East Riding Vol. 1: The City of Kingston upon Hull* (1969). Also substantial are E. Gillett and K.A. MacMahon, *A History of Hull* (2nd edn1989) and G. Jackson, *Hull in the 18th Century* (1972). For a short introduction to the setting, history, geography and more recent economic and planning history of the city see D. Spooner, *Discovering Cities: Kingston upon Hull*, Geographical Association (2005).

**Left:** The Deep Aquarium showing the 'Made In Hull' projection during the opening week of UK City of Culture, 2017. The Deep is located at the confluence of the River Hull and the Humber estuary.

# Acknowledgements

Majority text and revisions
by David and Susan Neave.

Deborah Wall of Historic England
and Philip Hampel of Hull City Council
oversaw the revision of the booklet.

Trevor Mitchell commented on draft text.

Thanks to the staff of Hull History Centre,
Hull Museums and Art Gallery,
Visit Hull and East Yorkshire,
Phil Haskins and Historic England Archives
for access to images for original edition.

Text:
© Historic England

Images:
© Historic England
Alun Bull: front cover, pages 2, 3, 6, 10 right, 19 top, 19
bottom, 21, 23 top, 23 bottom, 26 top, 29 left, 31, 35 right, 39
right, 43, 44
James O. Davies: page 37 right
Lucy Millson-Watkins: page 37 left
Bob Skingle: pages 14, 25, 30
?:13, 18, 35 left, 36 left, 36 right, 39 left

© British Library: page 5

© Philip Hampel: page 33 right

© Hull City Council/Hull Culture and Learning/Hull History
Centre: inside front cover, pages 4, 9, 10, 11 left, 11 right,
15 right, 16 left, 22 right, 28, 34, 38, 47, back cover

© Hull News & Pictures Ltd: page 29 right

© PA Danny Lawson: page 33 left

© David and Susan Neave: pages 8, 12, 16 right, 17 right,
22 left, 24, 26 bottom, 27 bottom, 28 top, 41, 48

© Neil Nicklin: pages 7, 32, 40

© Alex Ramsey: page 17 left

© Visit Hull and East Yorkshire: pages 15 left, 27 top, 39 left

© Wykeland Group: page 42

Design and layout: John Vallender, Historic England

Print: Deborah Wall, Historic England

Published 2017 by Historic England in partnership with Hull
City Council. Reprinted with minor amendments 2018.

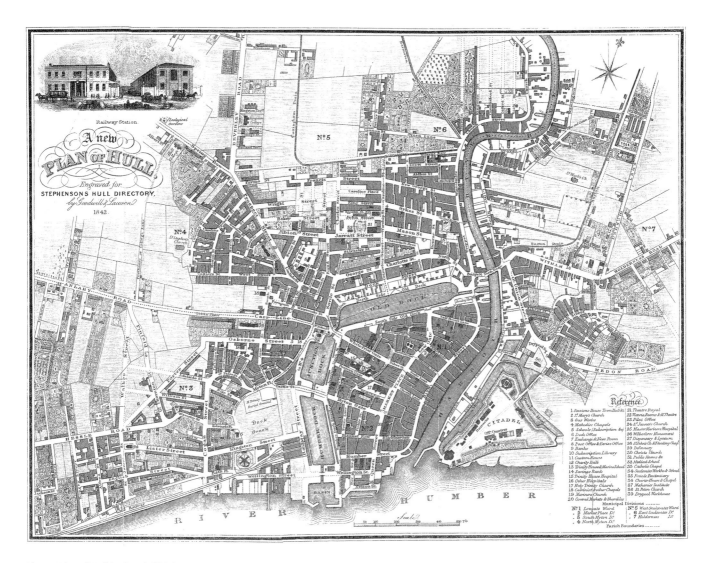

**Above:** Plan of Hull by Goodwill & Lawson, 1842.

**Above:** Hull from the Humber by Samuel and Nathaniel Buck, 1745.

## Key to plan

| | | | |
|---|---|---|---|
| 1 Site of Beverley Gate | 10 Georgian Houses | 19 King Billy Statue | 29 Pilot Office |
| 2 Blaydes House | 11 Guildhall | 20 Maister House | 30 St Charles Borromeo |
| 3 Charterhouse | 12 Hepworth's Arcade | 21 Maritime Museum | 31 St Mary's Church |
| 4 City Hall | 13 Hull Minster | 22 Trinity Market | 32 Scale Lane Footbridge |
| 5 Crowle House | 14 Hull and East Riding Museum (archaeology) | 23 Minerva Hotel | 33 Smoke House |
| 6 C4DI and Stage@TheDock | | 24 Old Dock Office | 34 Site of South Blockhouse |
| 7 The Deep | 15 Hull History Centre | 25 Old Grammar School | 35 Streetlife Museum |
| 8 Emigrant Waiting Room | 16 Hull New Theatre | 26 Paragon Arcade | 36 Tidal Surge Barrier |
| 9 Ferens Art Gallery | 17 Bonus Arena | 27 Paragon Interchange | 37 Trinity House |
| | 18 Humber Dock Marina | 28 Pease Warehouses | 38 Wilberforce House |